Changing and Empowering Lives Through Real Estate

A Conversation about the future.

By Lamont Johnson

ISBN: 978-0-578-90996-7

Dedication

This book is dedicated to the person who wants more out of life. Whether it's more money, better health, healthier relationships, more connected with their family, more opportunities, a more fulfilling job, a better car, better living arrangements, more cashflow, more investments, more peace, more balance, more control, more security, more conversations with God, or just more, and don't quite know what more is yet. More starts here, right now, today. In this book I talk about the foundation you need to get to the next level. Want to know what it is? Come talk to me, let's have a conversation. #AConversationAboutTheFuture

Table of Contents

who's backyard you run through, and which bush makes the best hiding spot. When I hid, I rarely got found. That's probably why I liked the game so much. My favorite part about the game was seeing one person chasing another heads up and it was just a matter of who was faster, or wanted to get away more. Neighborhood tag was so fun that we took the game from Beardsley, to my grandparents' house in Garden Hills, where we played with the kids in that neighborhood, just to find that we were still the best.

Everyone knew my favorite sport was basketball, but few knew my favorite game was Neighborhood Tag. Take five minutes to reflect on your favorite childhood game. Take the deepest breath you've ever taken. Inhale through your nose, hold it for 15 seconds, and exhale through your mouth. Think about the game that made you most happy, and think about why. Why was it your favorite game? Were you excited about who you got to play against? Was it good exercise? Where you the best at it? Take a second to take a jog down memory lane, and think about why that was your favorite game, also think about all the elements it took to make up that game. Who were you with? What did you have to wear? Where was this game played? You want to do these positive mental exercises a few times a day to train your brain to focus on things that makes you happy and put you in a good spirit. We will talk about it more later, for now let's talk about one of the triumphs I had to overcome growing up.

Younger days

I had the best childhood ever! I got everything I wanted: remote control cars, game systems, and scooters. My brother took me shopping for clothes in Chicago before the start of every school year. My God mom also kept me with the latest kicks. I ordered photos every year on picture day. when I turned 15, I was allowed to drive our Astro van to school. Reality is nothing more than how you view your circumstance, and the reality is, no matter how good my childhood was, I still grew up in a rough neighborhood.

One morning around 5 or 6, I was leaving my cousin's house on my new Mongoose with the mags and the pegs. Him and his neighbor shared a drive way. I rarely seen the neighbors outside, they didn't have any fancy cars, or huge additions on their house either. That morning as I sleepily rode my bike from my cousin's back yard to the driveway with my head down, I lifted my head and I was staring down the barrel of an AR-15. Once I was able to gather my thoughts, and was able to realize what was going on, I noticed there were about three more guns pointed at me with more guys moving in. I was in the middle of a SWAT team raid. The house my cousin shared a driveway with was being raided that's why they approached so quietly; they didn't want to alarm whoever was wanted. I've never had so many guns pointed at me in my life! I'm guessing my cousins called my family because next thing I know my grandpa was walking up cussing out the police for having their guns pointed at me. My dad and grandma had to hold him back because he was walking up to get me away from there, and their guns did not scare him. After my grandpa put up a fuss for a little the police quickly realized I wasn't coming from the house they were raiding and they let me go.

I was so young I didn't realize how big of a deal that event was. Growing up in my neighborhood those types of events happen all the time. I was just glad they didn't shoot me, and that's the problem. You should never be bombarded with guns drawn for a DWS. (Driving your bike While Sleep). That shouldn't be life, that shouldn't be normalized. In this new day and age, we are working towards normalizing luxury, plentifulness, and thriving instead of just surviving. We went through what we went through so the next generation don't have to. The next generation has to learn from our mistakes because they can't make them all. History repeats itself, that's why we have to share these kinds of experiences with our kids, and grandkids, so they can understand the severity of how far we have come. I admit we still have a long way to go but let's look at the glass half full: we can read, we can get married without our wives being raped in front of us, and then us whipped, we aren't being sold for money, we aren't being segregated, we have a lot of the same rights as everyone else in America, we can own real estate now, we can start businesses, and build generational wealth that we can transfer to our loved ones so they can keep moving the needle forward in bridging the wealth gap. Developing this mindset in my late 20s, changed the trajectory of my entire life!

Champaign to Mississippi

Growing up in Champaign, Illinois we had the best of both worlds. Our schools were integrated with some of the wealthiest families' kids, and some that weren't so wealthy. I was in the middle. A C- would have been my grade if we were graded by our family's bank account. I lived back and forwards between my grandparents' house and my mom, and we were far from rich but we never had money issues. My granddad was a hard-working farming man from Mississippi. I witnessed him slowly scrolling up to the house around 6 or 7pm daily after a long day of slaving on the back of an asphalt truck. He was an operator engineer. I saw him bring home $2,000 plus checks for one week. In my eyes, he was winning. Owned his home, good paying job, and a great marriage. His family is from Mississippi. As kids we would go down there once or twice a year for family reunions, and holidays. I loved the idea of having family from all around the country coming together to celebrate being a family. The family reunions were bigger than all the holidays combined. We would pack up our van, and sometimes an extra car and drive to Mississippi from Illinois and stay for a couple days. The drives went quick because as kids we slept most of the ride since we would leave around 2 or 3 in the mornings to arrive in the daytime. My great-grandmother, that we call "suga-ma" owns some land in Mississippi, so when we arrive, we would drive around this long rocky road until we got to the end of it, where Suga-ma's, and the only other three houses were for miles. When I went off to Mississippi my mom would jokingly say I came back an African from being in the sun, the Mississippi heat, and my whole body ate up from the world's biggest mosquitoes. At the family reunions we had more food than I've ever seen at any event in my life. There was barbeque grills, smokers, and picnic benches full of food. Even the breakfast meals for the weekend were the best. Tables full of bacon, eggs, grits, toast, and the like. It was truly a feast every time we visited Mississippi. It never felt like a visit though, the vibe was a home away from home. The energy, vibe, grace, were hitting on all pistons when we came together. The chemistry was at an all-time high in Mississippi. I loved it, however one of the things I didn't like so much was the animals you tend to get in the country parts of the south. One year we were down there visiting, and I seen the biggest snake I ever seen hanging from a tree. Some of the family looked at the snake and admired, some pointed, and I think someone went to go get it. I'm not sure because I didn't stick around to watch.

School Days

Growing up, my mom, older brother, and I lived all around Champaign-Urbana. I went to Garden hills for kindergarten. 1st through 3rd grade at Urbana's Wiley Elementary School. My 4th and 5th grade years were spent at Bottenfield Elementary School.

My first year of Middle School was spent at Jefferson until the actual night before 9/11 happened my house was burned down. It was the middle of the night and I was awakened to my step dad carrying me out a house full of smoke. We lived on fourth street, which honored my uncle because he served on city council. After the fire I went to my grandma's house and still went to school that next morning. I made it through a few classes that day then my dad came and got me out of school saying there was anthrax in the mail. I finished my first year of middle school at Jefferson, then went to Edison for 7th and 8th grade, where I started my basketball career. Although I had been playing since I was big enough to walk, I didn't start organized basketball until 7th grade, and played until my junior year in high school. I went to Champaign Central High School for all four years of high school. Throughout my entire k-12 years I never had a D or a F. I always made the honor roll, and I actually liked school. I liked it so much because I got it. A lot of people made it harder than it was. You show up, participate, follow directions, try, and do your homework and you will be successful. The older we got, the less opened minded we got. The more pessimistic we got. The inner child is where we go to spark creativity, so if you can tap into the enthusiasm you had in kindergarten, you will be just as motivated after you walk the stage and get that diploma.

A lot of my motivation to keep my grades up in high school came from my drive to play sports. I loved basketball, and I was pretty good. Playing since I could walk, religiously watching all basketball related content on TV, and reenacting all the moves we liked. Constantly playing, and evolving my game, playing against all different skill sets all around town, I developed a high basketball I.Q. I understood chemistry, cohesion, the flow of the game, momentum shifts, and the like. I was a streetball favorite. Organized basketball on the other hand was a whole different world. Always making the team I had what it took, but I lacked execution, and the mindset to slow the game down to my speed. In street ball I was always one to let the game come to me. In organized basketball if you're waiting for it to come to you, you'll be waiting a long time. You have to go get it in organized basketball. You have to have tenacity, grit, grind and be hungry. Organized basketball is a race against time, just as much as it's a race to score the most points. If you are racing against time, then there is no time to waste. In order to be a starter, you have to start the energy, start the momentum, start the snowball effect. I learned a lot from basketball though. Basketball teaches you discipline, hard work, sportsmanship, teamwork, leadership skills and the like. One of my favorite lessons was anticipation. We did a full day of drills on how the defender should anticipate the pass. It was an action verse reaction drill. It highlighted Newton's third law, for every action there is an opposite and equal reaction. Being quick on your feet, and thinking a few steps ahead, amongst others aren't even the tip of the iceberg of skills we learned playing basketball. Also, just getting active. A body in motion stays in motion, and exercise and staying active is very important. Being able to go outside and play every day gets taken for granted as a kid. Now that I'm older I wish I could carve out more time to be more active. As a kid it was part of my daily routine, but for the past few years it has been more of a challenge the way my work schedule was set up. Some days we worked 12–16-hour shifts, and it was some days I would come home and pass out in the hall way because I was over exerted and exhausted. I wouldn't even make it to my bed! This year exercise will be prioritized though.

After high school I started studying at our local community college, and it was surprisingly easy. That's where I actively stepped up my study habits, which stuck with me until this day. I would read the chapter, reread it and take notes the next time, then read it again. I figure if you can memorize the words to your favorite song, you can memorize the context of a course book. At the community college I studied Mass Communication, which later became just Communication. It was a major where you could become a music producer, video editor, journalist, reporter, radio talent, basically anything in the entertainment field. The classes were extremely easy. The test was from home, open book, and if you got an answer wrong you could just turn around and take the test over, with the same questions and answers and get a 100%. There was no reason not to get 100% on every test. I felt like it was either too easy for all the hype around "going to college", or I was too big for it, and had bigger dreams, goals, and ambitions. I didn't finish college because every opportunity I got to work I took it, even if it involved putting school on the back burner because it was so easy. For example, I was taking video production 101 and they taught us about the local free public access networks, and how you can get your productions on them as long as your show is educational or informational. Facebook videos was just getting popular, and I was doing a lot of recording for my friends and editing their music videos. I was able to get them to our public access station because those videos quickly let to a TV show I called "Kicking It Wit Mont". My favorite episode was The Evolution of Dance, where I highlighted some of the most popular dances dating as far back as the early 80s. I worked on my TV show amongst other things, and didn't go back to school that semester. At the time my high school sweet heart and I had gotten our first apartment together. A 1-bedroom apartment with paid utilities for $525 a month, couldn't beat it. I was working at TJ Maxx and I had recently helped a guy start a clothing store that is still there today. It was funny how I met them. I was walking from Spalding Park, from playing basketball with the guys. I had on some fresh Nike Jordan Fusions and a nice outfit. That was back when we wore our basketball shorts under out jeans. An older Arabian man pulled up next to me and slowly rolled down his window, and told me to come here. I was weary because of the neighborhood, but in my neighborhood, you can't show any fear, so because something felt off, and I knew most people wouldn't have walked up to the SUV, I displayed my tough side and walked up to them real cool and held a conversation with them. Turns out they was working on opening a clothing store in Champaign, and he just liked the way I dressed and wanted me to help them pick a location because I was from Champaign. I drove around a little bit and found a prime location. At the time I didn't know anything about foot traffic, or easy access, but I chose a store front on the corner of Bloomington and Prospect, which was later turned into a beauty supply store. They ended up choosing a store front that was right across the street from the building I chose. They named the store Active Wear, and it is still up and running today. A couple of buddies and I did all the work getting the store ready, from the paint, to hanging hooks, and building counters and the like. I designed the flyers, but it wasn't an up-to-date flyer so they had someone else design one, but I still passed them out. I worked in Active Wear nights after I left TJ Maxx. I even got my girlfriend involved, and she got really close with the owners as well. From selling my Kicking it Wit Mont DVDs out of Active Wear, and knowing a nice number of the shoppers, the owners were quickly ready to open another location. We opened a store in Urbana right next to the old Home Run, and we called it Exclusive Fashion. Looking back, I can tell they wanted to give me that store. They were real adamant about me learning all the logistics and the behind-the-scenes stuff, like ordering more inventory, who we order it from, how much to order, and the like. Not understanding financial literacy at the time, I didn't want to do anything more than what I was getting paid for, and that created a little tension. Exclusive Fashion didn't last more than a few months and I was back to working a few hours here and there in Active Wear during peak season.

After Exclusive Fashion went out of business, I was still working TJ Maxx, and went back to working my very first job which was Sonics Drive-in. During the time I juggled the 3 jobs and tried to go back to school. One of the classes I was taking was a sports class, teaching us about basketball. They taught us about all the different leagues, and I learned that Chicago which was only 2 hours away had a D-league team. After emailing the coach of one of the Chicago D-league teams for 2 months, I was invited to one of the tryouts. I had just bought a 1988 Chevy Caprice Classic. It had chrome 24-inch rims, and I drove it right to Chicago, pot holes and all. Tryouts lasted for a few weeks and I eventually made the team. I had a max contract earning a certain amount per game. The feeling was incredible. We had practice three times a week, and sometimes when I got there early, I would get a hotel room. I felt like I was living the NBA lifestyle. Getting paid to do something you love and something you've been doing your entire life, is like a dream come true. If I would have had the mindset I have now I would have made it work. At the time I justified me walking away from the team because I was traveling from Champaign to Chicago 3 times a week for practice, surviving off a minimum wage job and no savings account.

I broke up with my girlfriend at the time, moved back with my grandparents, dropped out of school, and on top of that lost my job at TJ Maxx. It was like a mid-life crisis, mixed with depression, sprinkled with a lot of bad luck. To make matters even worse my only source of income was a paper route. On June 12,2013 I was 23 years old and my mom passed from cancer. It felt like the world had stopped spinning. To know me was to know I was a momma's boy. Out of every check I ever earned I would give my mom some money, buy her something, or do something nice for her. My entire world evolved around her. I feel like my whole purpose was to make her proud of me and disappointing my mom was the worst thing I could do. When she passed, I felt like all eyes was on me, everyone was looking to me to see how I handled the situation, so for that I tried to overcompensate for the hurt I endured by being strong. The harder I tried to be strong the more I veered away from the truth. Tears are the way to cleanse the soul, and I didn't get my soul clean until 2 years later when my grandma passed on the same day of the year that my mom had passed. The one word that comes to mind when I think about my mom passing was disbelief. Optimism only goes so far and sometimes you eventually have to face reality, and I never came around. It felt like a bad dream that I had had one too many times. I just wanted my mom to jump out at me from around a corner, and scare me and tell me it was all a joke and she was alright. What really put me over the top was going to my mom's funeral. It took a lot out of me to go to the funeral because I'm not a funeral person. I didn't even want to be a Paul bearer. I was confused and offended when my brother asked me to be a Paul bearer. My mom just passed; the world is getting ready to end why would you even ask me that. Looking back, I wish I would have done it, and I'm extremely thankful to everyone who stepped up.

My aunt Diane rode with me to my mom's funeral. My oldest brother Terry and his daughters were the only ones there. Diane and I sat front row. It was like my mom knew I had walked in because I saw her twitch, or some sort of muscle movement, or something and from that moment you couldn't convince me my mom was really gone. I didn't even stay at the funeral. I left thinking: I don't have time for these games, she's not gone, ok I get it, I will get my life together. I masked my emotions by working. Outside looking in, you couldn't tell I was hurt, but there still isn't a day that goes by that I don't think about her. I contemplate too long on her memories I can drop a few tears at the blink of an eye. At the time I was working at Plastipak a bottle making factory through a temp service. I knew most of the shift leaders, and trainers and they allowed me to work as many hours as I wanted to. I worked there for 2 years, and in that 2-year span I worked 30 days straight 3 times. Granite some of the shifts were just 4 hour shifts to cover someone on my off day but I clocked in 30 days straight. My normal shift was 7am to 7pm, so it wasn't uncommon for 7pm to roll around and someone call off, or they were short on the night shift, and I would always volunteer to stay. That's how I ended up working a lot of 16 hour shifts but I worked about 3 24 hour shifts as well. I credit all the hours I worked at Plastipak to what got me my union job as an Ironworker. I was in Plastipak on lunch one day reading the paper and I saw an ad that said they were paying $20 an hour. At the time I didn't even know what Ironworking was, but for $20 an hour I could learn. I applied for the job and 3 months' worth of interviews later, I went from making minimum wage to $20.74 an hour.

Figuring it All Out

Starting what I felt like was my first career as an Ironworker January 2015 was extremely exciting. I hadn't been that proud since I had made the D-league Chicago Steam basketball team. It was a whole new world and not knowing what I was doing was the hardest part. My granddad was a union worker and I grew up watching him work on cars and stuff around the house so I had a basic knowledge of tools and how to use them. As far as mechanicals, or fixing basic things like small engines, I was clueless. Although I was willing to learn, I wanted to learn how I wanted to learn not how some Ironworkers wanted to train me. I just wasn't use to that type of environment.

On June 12, 2015 my grandmother passed, the same day of the year my mom had passed 2 years earlier. I was working the night shift, 7pm to 7am at the Hoopeston caning factory. Like normal I tried to hide my emotions behind my work. The night before my grandmother's homegoing, I went to work. I got off at 7 am with just enough time to shower and head to the church. Afterwards while everyone was eating, I left early to go take a hour nap and get ready to go back to work. This time was different though. I couldn't stop the water works. I was crying what my cousin calls them ugly tears, the whole day. She passed from Alzheimer's and she was better off on the other side because she couldn't remember anyone except my grandpa. That was beside the point though, I wanted her here with me. It just seemed like there was so much more the doctors and nurses could have done to keep her around a little while longer.

I lived with my grandpa for about 2 more years, then I finally moved out on my own. I moved to Urbana into a 3-bedroom, 1 bathroom, 1 car garage house. It had an added den, and about 1,300 square foot total. I called it the white house because, for one, it was white, and two, I felt presidential living in such a huge house by myself. It was a rent-to-own house which I put about $3,700 down on. I was paying $795 a month. I lived there for 6 months and talked to the landlord about getting out of my lease. He said it was fine but I wouldn't be getting my deposit back. I said that was fine and moved to some apartments on the other side of town called Mattis North. I caught a sweet deal. I was paying $595 for a 2-bedroom 1-bathroom apartment. I figured the move would free up some money and I would be able to save some money and get ahead. That was so far from the truth. It furthers the argument, the more you earn, the more you spend. Mattis North apartments is where I was living when I started my financial literacy journey, which I will talk about later in this book. I wasn't getting ahead, I wasn't saving any money, the move had been a complete waste of time. One day when I was at my grandpa's house, I asked him, "Papa, can I get my room back?"

He asked, "Why what's wrong?"

I said, "Nothing, I'm just tired of paying rent."

Then he said "Yeah, there isn't anyone back the".

That's how I moved back with my grandparents, for about the 6th time. My game plan was to live there just long enough to save up $30,000 and buy a house in that same area. As I was doing my research, checking Zillow, and googling matters related to home ownership, The Jay Morrison Academy ads came across my screen. King Jay Morrison was a great teacher. He was breaking down subjects into terms that I could understand, and most importantly relate to. He taught subjects on real estate, business, and credit. His school, (which was 100% online at the time, and since has moved into The Legacy Center in Atlanta GA) The Jay Morrison Academy, called it the RBC's, referencing the ABC's and how essential the subjects are. I quickly went to YouTube and watched ALL of King Jay's videos and the credit instructor King Will Roundtree's videos on YouTube and took thorough notes. After my YouTube spiral, I invested into the academy. In the academy I learned the principles of investing, business formation, credit building strategies, leverage, and the like. I learned that there are many ways to purchase a property besides cash. Shortly after investing into the academy, I went on to buy my first house, which was my first 6-figure deal, but I still wasn't satisfied, I still wasn't sold. I don't know if the knowledge came too easy, it was too good to be true, but like King Jay always says assume nothing, and verify everything. For that reason, I had to do some fact checking. I took the Illinois pre-broker's course to see how much of King Jay's teaching was legit, and everything was checking out. I passed my courses with nice recommendations from my instructor, who almost a year later, I went on and got sponsored by. That's when the real education started. If I was serious about real estate, I had to learn the ins and outs. The more you learn the more you earn, and I had no idea real estate would become more than a passion, it would become a calling. In order to fulfill my calling, and start walking in my purpose it's imperative I learn every aspect of real estate. Becoming a member of the Matt Difanis Team I will do just that, learn everything there is to learn, and learn how to do it correctly. I call Matt the real estate bible. After I went on my first few showings with Matt, I instantly started studying all the 5a (2) items of our contract. Being a real estate agent is not a team sport. You earn more money being a single agent, unless you are the owner of the team, and have agents working under you. That's the mindset shift I'm going to talk about later. We have to change our mindset from inspiring to be in the NBA to owning the NBA. Out of my entire life I've never heard anyone say they wanted to own a professional sports team, we always just wanted to play on one. Business however, is a team sport. No one builds a successful business alone. King Jay always says we should be the expert at hiring experts. When I was working 9-5s I never viewed it as me being hired to work, I always looked at it like I was hiring my bosses and giving them a chance to train me. Take school for example, when a student fails did he fail really or did the teacher fail at keeping him interested. That was my train of thought when I joined the Matt Difanis team. I already knew what he brought to the table, the question was what could I bring to the table. It would take someone as skilled as Matt to coach me up and bring the best out of me. A good partnership is an even swap no swindle, meaning, both sides benefit equally. It was a business decision to join the Matt Difanis team. A successful business has 7 sources of income, and I don't plan on profits from being a Realtor® to be my main source of income. I'm an investor. I invest not only money, but time, energy, and effort into my business. Investing into the best coaching for a few years, to set up my real estate career for life is a small price to pay.

If He Did it For Me, He Can Do It For You

I tell you my story so you can see anyone can do it. By it, I mean achieve your dreams, accomplish your goals, run up a bag. For whatever it's worth you still may need to find your dream, find your passion, come up with some goals, I'm very transparent so that you can see anyone can do it. I never knew real estate was my passion a few years back, when my only source of income was a paper route that I had to wake up at 1am every morning to deliver papers for two weeks just to get a $50 check. I didn't know real estate was even an option, I didn't know everything was real estate. I had no clue I'd be doing real estate. People don't know what they want until they know what they can have, and any career thinking or using my brain has never even been considered. All I knew was working hard, blood, sweat and tears with my hands, the harder you work the more money you make. The highest earners are critical thinkers, the ones who solve the most problems. The more you learn the more you earn in real estate, and I never in a million years would have predicted this would be my profession. I was just patient and failed my way into it. The definition of success is going from failure to failure and not losing momentum, so be patient, keep failing, and it will come to you. Philippians 4:6-7 says "do not be anxious about anything, but in every situation, by prayer and petition, with thanksgiving, present your request to God. And the peace of God, which transcends all understanding, will guard your hearts and your mind in Jesus Christ". In short

Chapter 2: Real Estate Theory

What Is Real Estate?

real es•tate

/'ré(ə)l əs,tát/

In short, my definition of real estate is everywhere. One of my virtual mentors does an exercise when he does his live events. He starts off by saying, "by a show of hands, who here lives somewhere?" Everyone has to raise their hand because unless you're homeless, you obviously live somewhere. Then he goes on to say, "well you're in real estate". He goes on to say real estate is everywhere, and we're all in real estate whether we're an owner or investor, then he talks about the pros and cons of owning and investing, which I will talk about later in this chapter. I know what you're thinking, people wouldn't have to raise their hands if they are homeless, but one of the worst quotes I've heard is, "if you don't own your home, you're homeless". This is a debate I have oh too often. Most agree if you are renting then you don't own your home, unless you are a great tenant and you treat your apartment or house like a home, because some landlords can give you the option to turn that apartment into a condo, or rent to own that house. Some say soon as you close on a house even, if you have a mortgage, (the agreement you make with the bank to pay them back because they bought the house for you) are the owner. It's me, I'm some. I say as soon as you close on a house regardless if you pay cash or get a mortage, you own the home and start reaping the benefits of being a home owner. If you take someone out to eat and buy their meal, and they promise to pay you back, is it not their food, or is it still your food until they pay you back? Some make the argument that it's not your house until you pay off the mortgage.

My rebuttal for that is, "if that's the case then we NEVER own the house for the simple fact that we will always pay taxes on the property and the land. We can't pay off our taxes, so since we will always be making those payments to the government does that mean we will never be home owners? I recently sold my Decatur portfolio which I didn't have a mortgage on any of the houses, but owning them felt the same as the ones I have mortgages on. When you become a home owner you definitely are on a new level. You have a new sense of belonging and pride. You walk with your chest held high and your life becomes just that much meaningful.

Wiki defines real estate as property consisting of land and the buildings on it, along with its natural resources such as crops, minerals or water, immovable property of this nature. Real estate is different from personal property which is not permanently attached to the land such as vehicles, boats, jewelry, furniture, tools, and the rolling stock of an agricultural farm. When you own a house, you typically own the land beneath it down to the center of the earth, the structure, and the air above the house up to infinity. In bigger city's air rights are subject to the property you are buying. God isn't making any more land, so the person who owns the most land wins. 10% of Americans own 88% of the land. 75% of white households own their home verses 44% of black households owning their home. According to the CFPB, black borrowers' share of home-purchase loans increased from 6.7% in 2018 to 7% in 2019 which was the 6th consecutive year increase. In 2019 Asian borrowers continued to take out loans with the largest loan amount averaging approximately $412,000 for home purchases. On the other hand, black borrowers continued to take out loans with the smallest loan amounts averaging approximately $243,000 for home purchases. The denial rate for conventional home-purchase loans were 16% for black borrowers. In contrast denial rates for such loans were 5.6% for Asian borrowers and 6.1% for white borrowers. According to the Federal Reserve, in 2017 predominantly non-white neighborhoods has a median credit score of 600 or lower. In comparison predominantly white areas had median credit scores of 660 or less. The scale is tipped, and not in the favor of blacks because for 400 years we weren't allowed to own real estate. We weren't allowed to do a lot of stuff for that matter, like read, write, eat normal foods, or get married. In slave days if a slave owner found out a couple of slaves had gotten married the slave owner would rape the wife in front of the husband and make him watch. The slave owner would then whip the husband and kill him or sell him. In books like Breaking the Chains of Psychological Slavery by Na'im Akbar, or Message in the Bottle the 40oz Scandal by Alfred Powell, they talk about how after slaves had learned to read, they were given the bible in order to make them feel better about being enslaved. I'm a Christian man I believe Jesus Christ died on a cross to save us from our sins. I'm pro Christianity, but I'm not against any other beliefs. Whatever you believe in, is whatever you believe in, and throughout this book you will hear me quote some bible verses like "If you sell land to one of your countrymen or buy any from him, do not take advantage of each other", Leviticus 25:14. That was actually the verse I had loaded for the first time I ever closed on a property. I was so appreciative and grateful that verse went well with the speech I had prepared. Not knowing what it would be like closing on a property going in, I didn't get to say my speech for two reasons: one, the sellers didn't even show up, and two I would have embarrassed the hell out of myself because every just wanted to get out of there.

Real estate is everything from single family homes, apartment buildings, hospitals, churches, schools, malls, strip malls, gas stations, storage units, stores restaurants, and the like. Streets, roads, alleys and highways are real estate. Although parks are sometimes owned by park districts, they are real estate too, that's why my virtual mentor says "Everything is real estate".

There's more than one type of real estate. The two that we see most are residential and commercial. Residential is a single-family house from one to four units. A duplex is considered a single family, a triplex, and a quadplex are single family houses. Five units or more are considered commercial real estate. Commercial also consist of apartment buildings, sky-scrapers, mixed use (store fronts with condos above or any combination), strip malls, stores, hospitals, hotels, and the like. Industrial warehousing often times are forgotten when considering commercial real estate. A few examples of industrial are warehouses, power plants, junk yards, coal plants, steel plants and the like.

Real estate is an asset, which means it goes up in value. In the real estate world, we call that appreciation. Appreciation can be a derivative of inflation. Inflation is when prices and values go up to compete with other countries. A good scale to base inflation is 3% yearly. There's also forced appreciation. When you buy your house and force the value to go up. There are a number of ways to do it but the most common way is to upgrade your house, repair some stuff in your house, or add on to your house. A realtor or an appraiser can give you some ideas of what items will add value. Everything you do will not give you a dollar-for-dollar return. If you do an upgrade now, depending on when you decide to sell, the value of the upgrade will decrease. For example, say you do a $20K (K means thousands) rehab on your bathroom. You'd use the bathrooms in your comparable properties to determine how much it will raise the value of your house. If you were to sell the house within two or three months the bathroom rehab could potentially raise the value of the house $5K-$10K. Again, I want to stress the fact these are random numbers and each property needs to be evaluated individually. In your market a $20K rehab can warrant a

$40K value increase. Another way to force appreciation is to have your neighbors fix up their houses. It's two ways to get the tallest building in the town. You can tear everyone else's building down, or you can put in the work to build yours up to be the tallest building. That's like the reverse to this strategy. If you can get all the neighbors to fix up their properties, that will raise the ARV (after repair value) of your rehab. Real estate also depreciates as well, and that is when it goes down in value. If you're a savvy investor with multiple properties or have a good tax strategist depreciation can be beneficial in certain situations. I see the most depreciation in vacant properties. If you do routine maintenance chances are your property will appreciate.

Developing Your Why

Real estate appreciates, and that's one of the top reasons why people want to own it. Understanding your why is one of the most important sections of the book right after the mindset. Without the right mindset your why won't get you far, but if you don't understand your why, the first road block you run into will knock you down. You can always determine the size of a man by the size of the obstacle it takes to knock him down. If your why is strong enough, and your mind is already made, no obstacle will stop you from accomplishing any goals not just owning real estate. The best exercise to determine why you are doing something is an exercise we call seven layers of why. It's quite simple we ask you why do you want to do something, and for the sake of this book I'll ask why do you want to own real estate. The first answer you gave is never the true answer, it's usually an answer you have locked and loaded, and rehearsed, ready to give to someone. It could also be the first thing that comes to mind, or the cool, in style answer to give, so we dive deeper than that. After you give your first answer, we ask why to that. If you first answer is "to leave something to my kids", then my next why will be "why is leaving something for your kids important?" Then we go back and forwards, you answering, and me asking why for 7 layers until we get to your real why.

My why, to becoming a homeowner was multiple reasons. Growing up sharing rooms with my older brother, all I ever wanted was my own room when I got older, so to become a home owner exceeded my expectations. It wasn't too many homeowners in my immediate family, so to become a homeowner I was drifting into uncharted territory. If I was to ever have kids, I will already have some assets to leave them. A wise man once said buy a rental property for every kid you have. Get a 15-year mortgage, and keep it rented out. When the 15 years are up and you own it out right, sell it and use the proceeds to pay for your kids to go to college. Owning real estate was about a status and class. Owning a home and having a high paying job was the old American dream, so I figured after I owned my house, I had made it, but when you're ambitious and accomplish a goal, you gain two more goals. Now I can add home owner and landlord to my titles. My why for owning real estate was the challenges I would have to overcome. If you want to make more money you have to solve more problems, so I use to get excited when people would complain about the struggles of owning a house. Some of the complaints I hear the most are, you have to cut the yard. Yes, that's true, if you own a house you have to cut the grass. Most of the time when you rent a house you have to cut the grass as well unless you're going to live in apartments all your life, or find land lords whose lease include lawn care. If you don't want to cut grass that's fine, you don't have to, HIRE someone. When I was a kid one of my first jobs was cutting grass. I was about 13 years old, and I don't know what I was more proud of, getting the $20 check, or the hunt. We were driving for dollars before we even knew what it was. We would walk, or ride our bikes around the neighborhood and look for yards that clearly needed to be cut. Once we found a yard with tall grass, but not too tall for our push mower, we'd go knock on the door and ask if we could cut their grass for a small fee. If they said no, we'd move on, if they said yes, we had a customer, but if no one answered we would always follow up. If you want to own a house but don't want to cut the grass that would be the perfect punishment if your kids get in trouble. Ask around the family, maybe your niece or nephew wants to make a few extra bucks. Whatever the case may be, don't not buy your house because you don't want to cut the grass. If you hire someone to do it you can create a job for someone who probably isn't old enough to find work elsewhere, and or build a lasting relationship. Another excuse I hear a lot is "What if something breaks?". Yes, you have to save up a few dollars for emergencies. If you have more than $2,000 in the bank you have more than the average American, and that has to change. I will discuss it more in the credit chapter but, we should have at least $10K-$15K in lines of credit for emergencies. If we have a credit card with a $10K-$15K credit limit, we will be ready for any emergency that comes up. If you're saving a few hundred dollars a month for owning a house verses renting you can put that in a special repairs savings account. After you first buy a house, you have the option to get a home owners warranty. All warranties are different and you can purchase different items with your warranty, but a typical warranty will cover items like HVAC, plumbing, electrical, and the like for 13 months. So, for those 13 months you're not worried about anything breaking because you're covered, you can be saving up. If you don't have a nest egg, it could be beneficial to reach out to someone so you can get put on a 1–2-year game plan to home ownership. Negative people have an excuse for every solution, and when I hear those excuses and realize it's no changing their minds, I remember home ownership really isn't for everyone, and that drives me too.

When I first started understanding the power of homeownership, and realizing I knew a little more than the average person I developed a love for real estate. I felt like the information was hoarded from us. When I say us, I mean anyone whose parents didn't have the means to educate them on financial literacy. Since financial literacy wasn't taught in school, the only way we could learn it was at home. Although I didn't learn the financial literacy basics until my late 20s, a lot of people still don't understand it. Some understand it and just don't apply it, and to know and not do is just as bad as not knowing. When I learned about financial literacy, I felt like I was part of the in-crowd. It's the being able to sit down with millionaires and add value to the conversation for me. That's a feeling I seek more of, which I will talk more about in the mindset chapter.

One of the main reasons people own real estate is for monetary reasons. When I was doing rent-to-own they wanted $67,000 for the house I was planning on buying. I put down $3,700 because I paid one month ahead, and I was paying $795 a month. If I was to buy that same house with a FHA loan at 3.5% down that would only be about $2,345 plus closing cost fees and taxes. My monthly payment would be about $400 a month. Not counting down-payment savings, I would save about $395 a month just by owning that same house instead of renting it. That's $4,740 a year. That's a little under $100,000 of savings in 20 years. The other side of that coin is: that's $100,000 more you'll pay to rent a house for 20 years verses owning that same house. Now my math isn't the best, but with $100,000 I think you can fix a few blown light bulbs or broken windows. That's just the tip of the iceberg. You get tax benefits for being a home owner as well. There's also appreciation and equity. Your house goes up in value, and equity is the difference in what you owe on the house and what the house is worth. For example: if you buy a $300,000 house, and in 20 years you pay it down and only owe $100,000, you now have $200,000 of equity built up in that house. Now let's just say in 20 years the house appreciated $100,000, so now you have $300,000 of built-up equity in your home. Which you can now cash out, called a cash-out-refi. You can get a line of credit on that $300,000. A line of credit is like a loan except you only owe interest on the part you spend, and after you pay it back it's still there for you to spend again. A line of credit is like a credit card except there is no fee to take out cash. You can also sell your house, pay back that $100,000 you still owe to the bank and pocket the $400,000 of equity you had built up in the house. Live in that apartment for 20 years and try to sell it, you'd be lucky if you even get your deposit back. Now granite this was just an example, these numbers are not real, each house and bank are different. You want to talk to your banker and or realtor to determine the proper exit strategy for you.

Rent-to-own (RTO) is one I get all the time since I actually did a rent-to-own before. There's a time and a place for everything, but rent-to-own just doesn't fit my business model. Some investors love the strategy because they get their house sold, and collect rent in the meantime. The thing I hear they love most about it is they are collecting rents, and don't have to do any of the repairs. When you're doing rent-to-owns you're in charge of all the repairs most of the time, just depends on what agreement you come up with. As a tenant or leasee rent-to-own doesn't seem like a good idea for me because it's for you to get your credit in place. The point of rent-to-own is for you to rent until your credit is in position to purchase the house you're renting, and the landlord has to sell it to you. The only problem with that is you're paying about double the rent you would be paying if you were renting regularly and then just bought a better house. Also, when renting to own a lot of landlords don't even report your payments to the credit bureaus, so it's not really helping you build your credit. I'm definitely anti rent-to-own unless it fits your business plan, and you have the mindset for it.

Chapter 3: #MillionaireMindset

98% Mindset, 2% Mechanics

The mindset is the single most important factor when getting more out of life, accomplishing your goals, and even owning real estate. Most business owners will say their business is 98% mindset and 2% mechanics. That means we can teach you the business in a few hours, but if you don't have the mindset to apply the skills we show you, or execute you will not be successful. There are different types of mindsets, and principles you want to develop in order to be success. That list is never ending but a major principle is a positive mental attitude (PMA). The theory behind it is looking at the cup half full instead of half empty. If you are taking all the proper steps and actions to make an event happen, or see a certain outcome, you have to have faith in the law of the universe that if you put the work in the results will come. Tony Robbins does a skit that says you can't just close your eyes and say "There's no weeds in the garden, there's no weeds in the garden" and then all the weeds from the garden will be gone. Positive mental attitude doesn't work like that. Developing a positive mental attitude is the process of taking yourself, your emotions, and your feelings out of the situation and looking at the bigger picture. Being optimistic may or may not be a trait of someone with a PMA. You don't just walk around in a good mood all day just uppy and cheerful. In theory, that's how we would all love to be but life happens to us all. When life happens, and the pressure is on, PMA will have trained your brain on how you want to act in a situation or circumstance, because we don't rise to the occasion, we revert back to training. One of my favorite books on PMA is Napoleon Hill's Success Through a Positive Mental Attitude. Being able to control your emotions is another principle, T.D. Jakes calls it the emotion

skip out on a few holidays, pass up a couple birthdays, cancel Christmas a few years, just to put you in position to celebrate the right way for life. They have a name for that term it's called delayed gratification. It's when you prioritize now, so you can live comfortable later.

Financial Literacy

Financial literacy plays a huge part in developing the mindset you'll need to accomplish your goals. You don't know what you don't know, so most people don't know that they can leverage their credit and get a credit card, a loan, and personal line of credit at a bank. Say they are all for $10K, you just leveraged your credit to create $30K out of thin air, just by having your credit in position. That's just at one bank you can do that with 10 banks creating $300K of capitol. You can also do it with a business or LLC. Rinse and repeat with three LLCs and you have yourself a million dollars of business capital. I call it business capital because it should be used to invest. Invest in whatever medium or vehicle you prefer, just make sure your ROI is more than your APR and that's how you get the law of infinite returns. If everyone knew how easy it was to make money out of thin air, we would be operating out of a place of plentifulness instead of desperation, survival, or scarcity. It can be that simple if you know what you doing but if this is all new information to you I don't advice you to go try it yourself. You'll need a coach or mentor, which I will discuss later, an accountant, tax strategist, and lawyer, to name a few members on your team. Although it can be as simple as I explained, there are strategies to every step like how to remove the hard inquires, or liquidate the credit cards without paying a cash advance fee and the like. Financial literacy is definitely on the rise. In the early 90s, over-night successes were going broke within 2 years. When I say overnight success, I mean anyone who got a lot of money from one big check, like ball players, music artist, tv stars, etc. Success doesn't come over night, and they worked really hard to get to where they were, but they didn't study financial literacy so they turned to drugs, or was filing bankruptcy within 2 years. Now with financial awareness being on everyone's radar, when we come across some money, we're starting businesses, making movies, restaurants, trucking companies, buying real estate, making investments, getting stocks, crypto, bit coin, and the like. Now we are thinking way farther ahead than just a temporary satisfaction, we're building generational wealth, leaving a legacy, and investing in assets we can pass down for generations to come.

What is Financial Literacy

If you're serious about financial literacy you know it's a journey that lives on long after you. Insurance is the number one-way wealth is transferred from generation to generation, so if you build a legacy it will live on after you have gone home. The main subjects of financial literacy are real estate, business, credit, taxes, and insurance. I started my financial literacy journey around 2017 – 2018 when I was living in Mattis North apartments. A buddy of mine reached out because he seen on Facebook, I had been doing a lot of reading. He said he had an opportunity that would be perfect for me, and we could possibly make a lot of money. All I had to do was talk to his mentor. His mentor was great. He was extremely uplifting. He was so optimistic, and has such a positive outlook on life. We connected because we had read a few of the same Robert Kiyosaki books. We met a few more times, and eventually I started my first business. I sold soaps. I won't say for who but let's just say they may or may not own a basketball arena in Orlando. If you believe in your product your customers will believe in you, and I didn't whole heartedly believe in the soaps. I believed in the money it could make, because I seen it, but as far as the product actually helping people, the customers seen right through me. Safe to say that business didn't last long, but it wasn't the experience that stuck with me, it was the education and the environment. They not only taught financial literacy, they taught the success principles, and the mindset you need in order to sustain the finances after you get them. A few of the things that stuck with me until this day are the core values. Core was an acronym for change or remain employed. A Few of the core principles was to read at least 15 pages a day, and listen to an audio for at least 15 minutes. Although the richest people in the world read at least 2 hours a day, I still to this day make sure I read at least 15 minutes a day. Hopefully I eventually work my way up to 2 hours a day! That's not just reading any old novel. The law of the universe applies to the mind as well, what you put in your mind you get out. It was explained to me like a straw, whatever you stuff in one end of a straw, and keep stuffing and keep stuffing, eventually it will come out the other end. The first end of the straw being whatever you feed your brain, and it comes out through your actions, your conversation, how you walk, how you carry yourself, how you treat people, how you let people treat you, your prayer, your faith, your praise, etc. For that reason, I started researching money. Everything I could find about money! If I could put enough money in my head eventually, I could be making money in my sleep. I started with YouTube University. There was an actual Yale's economics class from start to finish, where they just sat a camera in the back for the entire course. I found the book online and ordered it as well. That class was taught by Robert Shiller and David Swensen. David Swensen took Yale from a 1-billion-dollar company in 1985 when he started working there, to a $29.4 billion dollar endowment in 2019. The class talked about everything financial related from GDPs, to foreign markets and how they correlate to our market on a macro level. I also found an accountant class at YouTube University which I took and took thorough notes. I started reading books like Creature from Jekyll Island. That is a great book if you want to learn about money. It tells you the history of money, how the dollar was originally a receipt for gold. It goes in depth about how in the early 1900s the president, Andrew Carnegie, Rockafellas, and a few others went to Jekyll Island and created the dollar. James Rickard book Currency Wars further supplemented the info about the money. I read Tony Robbins book Money Master the Game, cover to cover and it was the longest book I had ever read. It was about 600 pages, but it was about money and I was hanging on to every word! Rich Dad Poor Dad by Robert Kiyosaki Is a financial literacy must read. If you say you're studying financial literacy and you haven't read any of Robert Kiyosaki books, you aren't studying the right stuff. Robert Kiyosaki says you should attend at least 3 conferences a year, so when Tony Robbins came to town Chicago, I had to attend it. There were a ton of other people speaking too that I had heard of but it wasn't until that conference that I started following them, like Dean Graziosi, Kevin O'leary, and Gary Vaynerchuk. They are subscribed on YouTube so whenever they post something new, I get a notification. That same weekend I went from Chicago to Milwaukee because the credit God King Will Roundtree had an event as well. I first came across him when I was just looking at houses. I was looking at houses to buy cash because I was living with my grandparents, and was able to save up a couple of dollars. Through magical marketing, The Jay Morrison Academy came across my screen, and I researched all of King Will's and King Jays videos on YouTube. I watched every last video in its entirety, and took thorough notes. After that I bought into their program. The Jay Morrison Academy. In the academy they teach Real Estate, Business, and Credit, and call it the RBC's.

They say we should be taught these three subjects like we're taught our ABC's, so they called it the RBC's. The real estate trained us on how to invest in real estate, no money down deals, joint ventures, syndications, wholesaling, multi-family investing amongst others. The information made so much sense, I took the Illinois Pre-brokers courses just to do some fact checking, and I passed the class with flying colors. That's how I became a real estate agent with RE/MAX Realty Associates The Matt Difanis Team. Doing all this research about money I came across two things: one 90% of the rich and wealthy got their riches through real estate. Two, after you get the money, you have to have the right mindset in order to sustain it. There are certain principles that the rich and successful do in order to be successful and stay successful. I call them success principles. Those principles consist of reading daily, listening to audio books daily, maintaining a positive mental attitude, tithing 10% of your income, giving back/ practicing the law of the universe, exercising/eating healthy, and understanding financial literacy is huge in order to sustain your wealth.

The goal of financial literacy is obtaining financial freedom. Depending on who you ask, everyone has their own definition of financial freedom. I define it as wealth. How long can you survive without a check? The most important asset is time. You can get more money, you can fix your credit, you can get more partners, but you can't get more time. Owning your own time is a main focus of financial freedom.

What does it mean to own your time?

If you have to wake up at 5am, get dressed, be ready for work by 7 am, work until 5pm, then take 30 more minutes to drive home. If you have to stop for gas, or food, or by a relative's house to say hi, you've lost 13 hours of the day. I say you lost it because yes you earned a check, but it was a check from building someone else's dream. If it wasn't something you love to do, you didn't own those 13 hours. If you wake up on a Tuesday, and you or your kid is sick, are you afraid to tell your boss you aren't coming to work? When you own your time, you decide where you are going to be every day, and when you're going to be there. One of the ways people gain financial freedom is the millionaire rule. Most millionaires have 7 sources of income. I picked that rule apart, and even took it a step further, I say 7 sources of income with 7 sources of income. Now I say if you want a million-dollar business, you want to aim for 7 sources of income. Also, not just income, but passive income. If you don't know the difference between active income and passive income, it's simple; active income is trading time for money. You go to work, then you collect a check. Passive income is putting in the work once, then constantly reaping the benefits from that work. Example, if you make a movie and you get $2 per movie sale in perpetuity, you have created passive income, because you're not doing any more work, but you're still collecting those checks for the rest of your life.

Owning your time is huge, but it's hard. The ones that obtain it deserve it, they came from where we came from, they faced the same challenges we faced, but in order to get to that next level they did one thing, didn't quit!

Dream Again

The inner child is where a man goes to dream again. The ability to dream is a huge skill when developing a successful mindset. You don't want to just dream, dream big. If you know how to accomplish your dreams, you're not dreaming big enough. If you aim for the moon and miss, you still hit the stars, so you can't be afraid to dream, and dream big. Dreams are imperative when developing your mindset. If you have no dreams, you have no north star. Dreams and faith run hand-in-hand. The ability to dream is the ability to have faith that something so big can happen to change the trajectory of your life. If you are actively taking the steps towards achieving your goals it's that much easier to believe in your dreams because you are taking action, doing everything you can, and leaving the rest to the law of the universe. A big dream will guide you through your goals. When you face adversity when trying to accomplish a goal, if you have a dream, you can step back and evaluate the situation clearly. A dreamer understands we don't have to win every battle as long as we win the war. Kids dream the most. As a child we ask kids "What do you want to be when you grow up". Kids will shoot you a million different answers, doctors, lawyers, basketball players, movie stars, fire fighters, and the like. If you ask that same child how they will do it, they will either have no clue, or give a real vague answer. The how never crosses a child's mind, they just know they are going to be a firefighter one day. A child hears the word "no" 400 times a day, and it doesn't slow them down one bit. We have to learn how to keep that trait throughout life. Adults can hear "no" one time and give up. We tend to talk ourselves out of a dream just by having the wrong mindset. The Bible says life and death is in the power of the tongue, so when we start speaking negatively about our dreams, we start counting ourselves out before we even give the dreams a chance. When we come up with an idea, instinctively we ask ourself how will we accomplish this idea? The person who knows how works for the person who knows why. The idea should be enough to start moving forward. All it takes is faith of a mustard seed to move a mountain. Once we ask ourself "how" and don't have an answer we start telling ourselves it can't be done, and that's the equivalent to telling ourself no to even trying to achieve this dream, goal, or idea. As an adult, one "no" and it's back to the drawing board, but children hear “no” 400 times a day. What if we applied that same relentless and persistence to our adult life? In business and sales, they say success is in the 8th follow up. We have to hear no 7xs before we get a sale typically, so if we hear no and quit, we would never make it to that 7th “no” and eventually a sale on the 8th follow up. Imagine thinking like a child, and expecting to hear “no” 400xs before you got a “yes”, whatever your yes may be, a sale, some support, or winning a negotiation.

I worked at Plastipak for 2 years as line worker. It’s a plant that makes different types of bottles from pop bottles, mayo bottles, laundry detergent bottles, and the like. Over my 2-year span I was a work-a-holic. I worked 30 days straight 3 different times. Granite some of those days I just went in for 4-hour shifts, but I did go in. My scheduled shift was a 12-hour shift, but I worked plenty of 16 hour shifts and a few 24-hour shifts. Yes, I said 24-hour shifts. Working those long nights, reminded me of when I use to drive to Mississippi, leaving at like 2am. We found out 24-hour shifts aren’t even legal so they had to split up my hours into two different pay periods. I was either a great worker, or so willing to work they would let me come in, either way, they let me come in and work all the hours I wanted to. I was talking to one of my good friends Lee-Ann one day, and I was telling her how I was going to buy me a house. It was still in the preliminary stages so I didn’t have all the details worked out yet. Lee-Ann asked, “How are you going to buy a house working here?”

I was stuck, lost for words, because I never looked at it that way. I didn’t think about the how, so I didn’t have an answer to that. I didn’t think to say I won’t be working here forever, or saying I was going to get a raise, or saying my credit will one day be in position. That was one of the first times I realized everyone didn’t have the same goals and aspirations. Like money for example, everyone doesn’t want to be rich. Growing up I thought everyone had the same goals, get rich, and that's definitely not the case. A lot of people are ok living average lives, working average jobs, living average life-styles. Not me though, I don't feel like I'm living up to God's potential of I settle for less. The reaction I was looking for when I told Lee-Ann about me buying a house was excitement. Maybe a congratulations, or even some help or advice, but as soon as I told her about my goal, I got my first "no". I know how to dream, and know everyone will not understand the vision, or support the movement, because if I didn't, I would have put my head down and given up that day. I wouldn't have closed on over 7 no money down real estate deals, or I wouldn't have become a landlord, most importantly I wouldn't have become a homeowner. I also wouldn't have become a real estate agent so I could help others become homeowners as well. I actively practice dreaming big with exercises to train the brain. Your brain is a muscle if you don't exercise it, you can lose it. I train my brain to dream big with exercises like vision boards. I got two exercises from one of my virtual mentors. The first one, similar to a vision board, I wrote out a $1,000,000 check to myself, and dated it for 5 years down the line. To be able to feel it, look at it, hold it, is something more special than just saying one day I will make a million dollars. Coincidently, one of my clients closed on her house a few days after I wrote that check, and I was able to have both checks sitting by each other.

The next exercise was extremely fun to do, think about, and imagine. This is an exercise I want you to do as well. It's called the perfect day challenge. My mentor said his mentor had him do this exercise, and now I'm passing it down to you. In the exercise you have to write a letter to yourself describing what your perfect day looks like. Who are you with, what are you doing, how much money do you have, what kind of toys do you have, where you traveled, and the like. The idea of this exercise is to dream big. Most people know what they don't want, but few know what they want, that's why they never get it because they don't specify it. When I was writing this, it was difficult for me to get away from what I know. Looking back, my perfect day was something extremely tangible because I've seen it before. If I could do it over, I would have been living in outer space or something, feeding my pet alien. My mentor said after he wrote this letter, 6 months later, he was living his perfect day. My perfect day went like this:

My perfect day starts at 5am while everyone is still sleeping. I start my day off by going on a light jog to clear my mind, put me at ease, and have me relaxed all day. The Art of War says whoever is first in the field, and awaits the coming of the enemy, will be fresh for the fight. So on my ideal day I'd get up early and go on a jog by myself. Something slight, between a mile or two, around the lake that's in my back yard a few times.

After my jog it will be around 6am. On my perfect day I will return home, shower, and my wife or cook will have the perfect breakfast waiting on me. Bacon, eggs, chocolate pancakes, hash browns, and fried hot dogs. I'll wash it down with a big glass of orange juice, and wash that down with a nestle pure bottle water. A few grapes after that, just for the fruit. My house will be sitting on a bunch of acres, with a lake in the backyard. Most of the house is made of bullet proof glass, so I can eat my breakfast, and look out at the beautiful view of the lake. While eating breakfast I'll make a few posts to my social media accounts to say good morning to my family, before I head upstairs to say good morning to my wife and kids.

After saying good morning to all of my family, whether via social media, or the immediate family in the house, I hurry up and get dressed for all of my 8 o'clock conference calls. Calls with King Jay Morrison, King Issac Grace, King Will Roundtree, E.T. The Hip Hop

Preacher, Pastor Marlon Lock, T.D. Jakes, Dean Graziosi, Gary Vaynerchuk, Tony Robbins, Daymond John, Jay-Z, Mark Zuckerberg, Elon Musk, Robert Kiyosaki, Minister Farrakhan, Dame Dash, and a few others. We meet monthly for our mastermind calls, which I earned through an entrepreneur competition. Then I became family after they seen the vision, and believed in the vision. The masterminds always keep us up-to-date with market trends, and what's going on with billion-dollar industries, and companies. These masterminds let us know future, and projected trends, and how to become rich in these times. These masterminds tell us conflict resolution strategies, mindset training, problem solving, character building, and some of the best stories you will ever hear. Not too many people in the conference call spoke about their money, but Dame Dash spoke about his which made me go check my bank account.

After our two-hour conference call, which ended right at 10 o'clock, I checked my bank account: Dear lord, thank you for waking me up today. Blessing my family enough to where we are all in good health, we all have an overflow of food, and shelter. Thank you for controlling my tongue when I wanted to tell it like it is, but I don't because I know after someone talks to a Christian they should be in a better place. Thank you for covering me, and allowing me to walk in my purpose. Thank you for blessing me with this bank account. I used to be scared to pray for wants but James 4:2-3 says you have not because you ask not, so I started asking for wants too Lord. Lord continue to bless me, and water my seeds of faith. Lord continue to energize me, and give me courage to take these real estate risk. Also continue to flood my bank account with these 0s Lord. In Jesus name I pray, Amen.

That's the prayer I said after I checked my bank account and seen all the deposits from all 200 tenants, deposits from a commercial real estate sale, a deposit from some of my land, a deposit from my commercial tenants, a deposit from a few of my companies, a deposit from my book deal, and a deposit from my clothing line. After checking my bank account, I talked with the chief operating officer of my real estate holding companies. I directed him on what material to order from the hardware online store, so the maintenance man can pick it up in store, and install it in one of our rentals.

I get into my black, presidential Yukon Denali and head down to the office. After I get to the office, I ask our credit attorney some questions about the newest fico model, and assist our secretary with some property management advice. After hanging out in the office for a few hours I head out. As I'm leaving the secretary brags about how much revenue she has made up, music to my ears. As I get into the Denali to go pick up the Texas Roadhouse my wife called and ordered, I get a call from my brother T-bone saying him and my niece and nephew headed to my house to go fishing in my lake that's out back. I played that new 2chainz, and Jeezy to pick up the food. As I arrived home, the gate didn't open to let me in the driveway, for some reason it was broke. So, I had to manually get out and open the gate, as the dogs gathered around to greet me.

After lunch it was about 2:30 pm, so I went out to the lake to see how the fishing was going. Everyone had a bunch of fish and was bragging about how good they fish. I'm not the best fisherman in the world so I suggested we race four wheelers. We raced around the lake until Moon slow self drove into the lake. It took us about an hour to tow him out the lake. We were joking and making fun of him for not being a good driver, so he we getting loud and joking about how he was the best shooter, so I said, "The only way to solve this is paintballing".

Everyone agreed, and we split off into teams, and ran off to get our paintball equipment.

Once the guys left, after a paintballing, I went into the house to chill with the family and start my study session. Self-education and reading is one of the things I do daily to feel accomplished. They say if you're not growing, you're dying, so if I don't do anything else, I have to self-educate.

My perfect day started off with a morning jog to get my mind right. I do that at least three times a week.If I don't start off with a morning jog, then I'll do my homework, read, and do my mindset training and get it over with. There's only three preachers I can listen to on the daily, and that's T.D. Jakes, Pastor Marlon Lock, and E.T. The hip hop preacher. I usually listen to them on my way to the store or anytime I'm in the car, and that's my version of bible study, and connecting with God. That's something I feel like you should do on the daily. I rarely ever listen to music when I'm by myself. I read about mindset, leadership, PMA, money, and real estate. Napoleon Hill, Jim Rohn, John Maxwell to name a few of my favorite.

A few things I didn't write about in my perfect day was: traveling, shopping, jewelry, planes, boats, etc. I didn't go too far on my perfect day, got my mind right, handled some business, and chilled with family is my perfect day.

What's Your Religion?

Dreaming is a huge part of developing a positive mental attitude and the mindset needed in order to take your life to that next level. Dreaming can only take you so far, then you have to take action, action can only take you so far then you have to leave the rest up to God. I'm real big on religion. I'm a Christian man, but regardless of what you believe in or don't believe in that is your choice. Listening to the word or someone talking about the bible is one of my lifelines. If I'm having a bad day, in a rut or a bad mood, there are a few things I can listen to and get me back in the right state. Some of my money advisors, mindset coaches, or one of my pastors. Learning the bible is a huge accomplishment and shouldn't be taken lightly. I haven't read it in its entirety yet. I've actually only made it word for word to the book of Leviticus. As I was reading the bible, I would google any movie that related to the book I was reading and go check that movie out and read it. No matter which movie I watched or how many times I reviewed a certain book of the bible, it amazes me how the preachers extrapolate meaning and messages.

One of the bible verses that always helps keep a positive mindset, keep me goal setting, and dreaming big is Hebrews 11:1. It says faith is the substance of things hoped for and the evidence of things unseen. For me that means, if you didn't believe you could get more out of life you wouldn't be reading this book. Just because it isn't clear how a goal will be accomplished; you know it can be done or it would have been far-fetched to set it in the first place. One of my pastors say thank him in advance for what's yours to come. Praise him in the midst of your storm because whatever your problem is, it has already been taken care of. Praise him now because he doesn't come to the storm, he comes to the praise.

Understanding better days are coming, and trials and tribulations are just part of growth was huge, and it didn't happen overnight. It's definitely not an easy process. Quick disclaimer, I am not an expert in none of these areas. I'm just telling the story of what I have learned so far because that's one of the biggest mistakes of our community, the ones before us never passed on what they learned. There's the five year, ten-thousand-hour rule that says you're not an expert of a subject until you been working or studying in that field for five years on ten thousand hours, whichever comes first. This is a general quote, and certain circumstances can increase, or decrease the process. I am not qualified to give lending advice, underwriting guidelines, any legal advice etc. A lot of the info in this book will be a general concept, and random numbers, to give you an idea, the courage to get started, and the language to be able to hold an intelligent conversation with professionals, and ask the right questions to get you where you need to be. If I was to go through and have a real estate attorney, mortgage lenders, credit attorneys, tax strategist, seasoned high level real estate investors, title agents, insurance agents, and the like, go through and write a chapter (which I could because I have great relationships with a lot of them) it would go over a lot of ya'll heads, and water down the message I'm trying to deliver. Each one teach a few, and with this information I was able to buy my first house and invest in real estate, which changed my life. People ask for handouts, but don't want to put the work in you put in to get what you have. When people ask me for something I give them the information I had to get it, to get to the next level, to become a home owner, and to get my credit intact.

How to Develop the Mindset

How do you develop the mindset you will need to get to the next level? How do I believe in a higher power if I'm not religious? Is it too late for me to learn financial literacy, and if it's not, how do I learn it?

The answer is simple, change! In order for things to change you must change. The thing about people who don't want to change is, they don't want to change. You can't continue to do the same things you been doing and expect a change, that's actually the definition of stupidity. You have to start small, it's the small everyday habits that spur change, getting to the next level, and getting more out of life. The little things that are easy to do, and even easier not to do, and doing them will separate the winners from the losers, the dreamers from the action takers, the players from the critics. One of my mentors say "they don't make statues of critics" meaning, in order to do something great you have to get off your butt and go make it happen. Studies show in order for an addict to kick an addiction you have to change their environment. We are the same way. Consider yourself addicted to average, negative thinking, making excuses. They say you can make money or make excuses but you can't do both. In order to stop making excuses we have to get around people who don't make excuses. We have to actively get around people that are executing on a high level. Pay them if you have to. They aren't going to come looking for you. Surround yourself with people doing the things in life you want to do. Be open minded, open to change because God shakes things up before he changes them. If you hang around 5 millionaires you will become the 6th. If a person can make millions yearly, or even monthly, surely, they can give you the information to make a few hundred thousand. It's the little things like studying what they study, reading the types of books they read, and if you really want to take it to the next level or are blessed with the chance to pick their brain you want to think how they think and make decisions how they make decisions.

Once you learn how to change your mindset, change your thinking, and live in a constant state of growth, you will get to the next level, you will get your millions, or whatever your goals may be. It's that simple, it's no secret recipe to become a millionaire, or a positive thinker, you just have to do the everyday daily habits that separate the successful from the unsuccessful. Getting to the next level is 98% mindset and 2% mechanics, that's why the majority of the book is about developing the mindset you'll need to succeed in any field. The rest of the book is about the strategy 80% of self-made millionaires used to get rich, real estate. We start with a conversation about credit, even if real estate isn't your passion, if your credit is intact, you can invest and self-fund any dream you have.

Chapter 4: Credit Game

Credit Philosophy

I call it the credit game because that's exactly what it is, A GAME! They say learn the rules of the game and play them better than anyone else. So, once you learn the credit game, it's something you will actively strategies for the rest of your life. Credit is a tool the rich use to get wealthy. After you get your credit in position you can leverage it to buy a house, investment properties, bootstrap a business, working capital for a business, car, etc. One thing you can't get a loan for is stock. You have to be very strategic in order to get a loan for stocks, and it's possible, but so risky banks steer clear of it. For that reason, I don't talk stocks too much in this book although I love the concept, and believe it is a great investment strategy to build wealth. Look at the facts though, even Wall Street is real estate, emphasis on the street. The rich use an investment strategy called the law of infinite return. In short, that's when you get a $100,000 loan invest it to make $300,000 and pay back the $120,000 because you will have to pay interest. Since you didn't use any of your own money, all you used was your name, your credit and credentials, signature, and knowledge, to create $180,000. We call that creating money out of thin air. It's the exact opposite of what I was taught growing up. I was taught to never touch your credit, if you don't have the money don't buy it, and save as much as possible. Those trainings and teachings might have been the best thing to do back then, and also probably is the basis of where I am today. There's business credit, personal credit, family credit, and partnerships. Once you master personal credit you can learn to leverage business credit as well. In essence you can leverage your business and get a $20,000 loan, $20,000 line of credit, and a credit card with a $20,000 limit. Like I said earlier, you can use it to invest in your business, weather you need new kitchen appliances for a restaurant, as leverage when negotiating who covers distribution in a clothing company, hiring more help, ordering inventory, or covering overhead, as long as your return on investment is more than your annual percentage rate, you'll be good. That's some high-level financing and I don't recommend doing it on your own for the simple fact that, it's just the basics of the strategy. There are some fast learners who will not need their hand held and understands the concept, and will be able to take it and run with it. For everyone else make sure you have the proper guidance when performing these strategies. I can't stress it enough, I may make it sound easy, but it's like giving a baby a loaded gun, you could set yourself back decades if not properly executed. A blessing too soon is not a blessing at all, so make sure you invest into some coaching and mentorship.

So, what if you don't want to leverage your credit to invest, whether you still believe cash is king, or you're just not ready to move that fast and just want to take your life to the next level having a good credit score is imperative. You move different when you have good credit. You walk in the bank different; dealerships roll out the red carpet when they see an 800-credit score. Now they're calling you Mr. And Mrs. Your credit score is used to determine where you live. If you don't have enough money to afford a house in a certain neighborhood, and you don't have good credit, you just can't live in that neighborhood. Some jobs pull credit, most of them mandate you sign a slip giving them permission to pull your credit. Insurance premiums are based off a credit score, along with utilities, not to mention if you are renting and you have bad credit you will have to put down three times the deposit.

What is a FICO Score?

Although lending can be traced back to the beginning of mankind, in the early Middle Ages Christians were not allowed to lend money with interest. The bible forbade it. In those times only the Jews were allowed to lend money. They determined your ability to make payments by word of mouth, and visiting your house and stores you frequently shop at. As you can guess that didn't work out too well. In the early 1950s Bill Fair an engineer, and Earl Isaac a mathematician created an algorithm that can determine your credit worthiness called the FICO score. There are similar scoring systems and models, like the vantage score, which credit karma uses. Extremely similar, to the point if you use those scores to determine your credit score you will be in a very similar range. Your credit score ranges from 300-850, with 300 being the worse and 800 being the best. There are five factors that make up your credit score; payment history, utilization, length of history, new credit, and mix of credit.

Payment history makes up the biggest portion of your credit score. 35% of your credit score is determined by your payment history. Credit is defined as your ability to make payments on time over time, so as long as you pay your bills on time 35% of your score will positively affect you score. If you only focused on paying your bills on time, every time, within enough time you will have a fairly decent credit score. It's the awareness that gets everyone. If your credit score is not at the forefront of your mind, you can't actively build your credit. Growing up I was always taught to never use your credit for anything. I not only didn't use my credit, but I misused my credit. Credit was like a secretive thing no one discussed, so if I secretively didn't pay a bill and swept it under the rug no one would know right? Wrong!! You're only hurting yourself by not keeping credit at the front of your mind.

Utilization is the next factor that makes up 30% of your credit score. Your credit utilization is the amount of your revolving credit that you have used, and the lower the better. For example, if you have a credit card with a $1,000 limit and you spend $900, you have just put yourself at 90% utilization. Utilization is easy to remember because it's 30% of what makes up your credit score, and you want to stay under 30% utilization. We call it the divide-by-3 rule. Soon as you open that credit card with the $1,000 limit, you want to divide that limit by 3, and make $300 your new limit. Although it's a limit of $1,000 anytime you spend over that 30% threshold it starts to negatively impact your credit score. Revolving credit and installment are more terms you need to know. Revolving credit is credit when after you spend it, and pay it back, it's still there for you to spend again. Examples of revolving credit is credit cards and lines of credit. Installment credit are your regular loans with set, fixed payment amounts. Examples of installment loans are student loans, car payments, mortgages, and payday loans. Your credit utilization is based on revolving lines of credit only.

One way savvy investors mitigate high utilization is to pay to become authorized users on someone else's credit card with a high limit. Do your research, however there are websites that sell authorized users.

15% of your credit is based on your credit length. Your length of history is how long you have been building your credit. If you just started building your credit 3 months ago then it will have a negative impact on your credit score. The longer your history the better. If you have been able to make payments on time over time, for a long time it makes you more credit worthy. The top 800 club has on average 20 years length of history. As of right now, while we are still using the Fico 8 scoring model, there are tricks to having a short credit history. One of the ways to mitigate a short credit history is a strategy called piggybacking. That's when you get on someone's credit card as an authorized user. They will send an extra card out, and usually that card goes to the original owner, but you will be able to reap the benefits of all the credit history from that card. For example, if you only have 1 year of credit history and you get on your husband's credit card that he has had for 15 years, those 15 years of credit will report on your credit profile. That can be a two-edged sword. If the person whose card you get on has bad credit or misses one payment, that will report on your credit as well potentially hurting your score. The new Fico10 scoring model will make piggybacking obsolete.

10% of your credit is mix of credit. They want to see a variety of credit like, student loans, credit card, car payments, mortgages etc.

The last 10% of what makes up a credit score is new credit. They want to see you using the credit they lend you, plus applying for new credit.

Those are the factors that make up your Fico score, but it's your whole profile that is more important than just the score. Your credit profile consists of anything they can use to determine your credit worthiness. Items like old addresses, if you have a lot of addresses, they can deem you unstable and reject you for a loan. Hard inquires, and tradelines help make up your profile as well. The less hard inquiries the better, although 10% of your score is applying for new credit. The higher your credit score, the more a hard inquiry will hurt you. The top 800 clubbers have at least 21 tradelines. Tradelines are anything constantly reporting on your profile. Mortgage, credit cards, car loans, any payments that are reporting to the credit bureaus qualify as a tradeline. Even piggybacking is considered a tradeline for the moment. Where you work, how long you've been there, and banking information all are part of your credit profile.

Derogatory marks put a huge ding on your credit as well. If you didn't make your payments on time, it will report as a late payment, resulting in a decrease of your credit score. The higher the score, the more derogatory marks impact your score. If you have something go to collections, that will be a bad look towards your credit. When you don't pay a bill, and there's no activity on that bill for typically 90 days, the servicer of that debt will sell your debt to a collection agency for pennies on the dollar. The collection company then uses whatever strategy necessary to collect that debt from you. Typically, they will report it to the credit bureaus, which I will touch on in a second, and depending what the debt is they may even garnish your wages, which is the only time you should file bankruptcy by the way. An example of when something would go to collections is; you stop making payments on your Sprint phone. You now owe Sprint $300. For whatever reason, you don't pay that bill, and they sell it to a collections company for $75.

Sprint's train of thought is, they weren't going to get any money out of you at all, so getting about $75 is better than nothing. The collection company is professionals at collecting all of what's owed, so they feel like a $75 investment to make $300 is a good investment. If it's a government owed debt, they may even garnish your tax returns until it is paid. Even if the collections are paid in full or settled, they will still report on your credit report for 7 years from last date of activity.

Most derogatory marks last on your credit report for 7 years. Everything from an unpaid car payment, to student loans report on your report for 7 years. Bankruptcies last for on your report for 10 years, and hard inquiries last for 25 months.

An inquiry occurs anytime a lender pulls your credit to determine your credit worthiness. There are hard inquiries and soft inquiries. Hard inquiries happen when a lender pulls your credit. Hard inquiries show up on your credit report and depending on your credit score, after so many inquiries they can start to have an adverse effect on your score. Soft inquiries, sometimes referred to as soft pulls, usually occur when you pull your own credit through some credit monitoring service, or you go for a pre-approval. Soft inquiries don't typically show up in the average credit report, but if you request a full credit report from the bureaus, your soft pulls will show up on there.

Those are the major components that make up your credit score. But what if you don't have any of those things on your credit? You've never had anything in your name, you've never had your credit checked or pulled, and you've never had anything go to collections. Although it is rare in most cases, you can go to get your credit pulled, and not have any credit at all. That's called a ghost profile. Having no credit score at all. Believe it or not, a ghost profile is better than having bad credit. Ghost profiles are more common with teens and young adults. With bad credit you have to go through credit repair, or work diligently at getting your score up. With a ghost profile you can make a few simple changes and have good credit. For example; you can become an authorize on someone's credit card who has good history, or you can get you a secured credit card or loan. Having a secured loan means you leverage some sort of collateral to get the loan. In the case of a secured credit card, you would submit a check with your application for the amount you are applying for. If it's a $2,000 line of credit, you would submit a $2,000 check. The $2,000 would be held in an escrow account. Secured cards are for people who don't have the best credit, so they are more lenient, because if you don't pay the bill, they already have the money anyways. However, if you do pay the bill on time every time, typically for one year, you then get to get your $2,000 deposit back, or however much you applied for. Again, I want to stress the fact that every bank is different, I'm not trying to be a banker, and do the bankers job, I'm just informing you of an idea so you will have enough courage to go talk to bankers, Realtors ®, real estate attorneys, credit attorneys, title agents, and the like. After your year is up, or however long your bank agrees to and you go to get your deposit back they might have to do another hard inquiry before they give you your credit increase, and or give you your money back. I still have a secured credit card with only a $300 limit because I can't afford a hard inquiry. We both have our poker faces on, kind of playing chicken because they know I can't afford a hard inquiry. Once you understand the credit game, you can never go broke. Your demeanor and the way you carry yourself changes when you walk around with a credit card with a $10,000 limit. As you can see, your language even changes. I went from I can't afford it, to I can't afford a hard inquiry.

Credit Bureaus

Now that you understand what makes up a credit score, where can you go to find it at? The credit bureaus house the information that makes up your credit report. There are three main credit bureaus in the U.S., Experian, Equifax, and Transunion. They are three separate entities and all have separate information, and usually separate scores. Just because a bank reports some information to one bureau doesn't mean they have to report information to the other two. The credit bureaus are governed by the Fair Credit Reporting Act (FCRA), and the Fair Debt Collection Practices Act (FDCPA). If there is any information that is inaccurate on your credit report you can complain to the Federal Trades Commision (FTC), and they will refer to the FCRA or FDCPA and possibly have the information removed from your credit report. In lemans terms we call it credit repair, and people pay lots of money to get their credit cleaned up. There have been a lot of breaches to the bureaus, you have identity theft, and simple mistakes. For example, if you and your dad have the same name, and he faulted on a payment and it accidentally get puts on your credit report because his application didn't specify senior or junior, you will have to dispute that to get it off of your credit.

There are other credit monitoring services besides the credit bureaus. There are websites where you can get one free credit report per year. There are free credit monitoring apps and websites you can use to get your Vantage score. Your vantage score is close enough to your FICO score that it's ok to base your credit score on it. You can use websites like Credit Karma, and Credit Wise. If you use Credit Karma it only gives you your TransUnion and Equifax report. I see a lot of people using Credit Karma and then going over to Experian.com to get their free Experian score.

Chapter 5: Real Estate 101

Now that you've learned why to invest in real estate whether that's buying your first home, or buying an investment property. You've learned the mindset you need to get to the next level, and stay there. You've learned that credit is the foundation you need to get to the next level and never go broke again. Now let's learn about the strategy that 80% of the self-made millionaires and billionaires used to attain their riches; real estate. There are hundreds and hundreds of books out there about real estate. There are books in other languages that hasn't even been converted into English. This book should be the alley-oop to set you up to go read some of those, and continue your journey or road to home ownership. This book is not an all out how to, that gives you every scenario, and every small step and feeling. This book is for the person who has never seen anyone buy a house, and in some cases might not even know anyone who owns a house. If you do own your home and or come from a long line of home ownership, then this book is a refresher and updater. Information changes every 18 months, and you learn by repetition. Whatever the case may be, if you want more out of life, this book holds a few keys that will unlock the next level.

Getting Started

The next thing to do when purchasing a house is gathering your team. You have to be the expert at hiring experts. A few key players in a real estate purchase are real estate agents, bankers, real estate attorneys, title companies, contractors, appraisers, and inspectors. You can start with your bank and see if they refer you to any real estate agents that they regularly use. You want to vet at least 3 different experts in each field. What you want to do is call and have conversations with them. After reading this book you should have enough courage to call and get the conversation started. Ask as many questions as possible. You want to ask questions that allow you to get a feel for who they are and what they represent. Their experience matters, ask about how many transactions like yours have they done, ask for references, and call them. When assembling your team, you want to make sure they work well together, so when you hire someone ask them to refer you to other professionals that you still need on your team. This is more of the easy part, just striking up the conversation.

Talking to your bank or real estate professional should be your first point of contact. If you are going to pay cash for your house you will want a proof of funds (POF) letter to present to your real estate professional. If you are going to get a loan or a mortgage for your purchase you will want to present your pre-approval letter to your real estate professional.

I've put disclaimers all throughout this book because I can't stress enough the fact that I am not trying to be a banker, I don't want to do their job. I'm merely giving a general idea on the subject. It is not entirely correct but put into terms that will encourage the average person to take action, and start their journey.

Getting Funding

When getting approved for a mortgage you have to have fairly decent credit. All banks have different guidelines, and post Covid they tightened up on their lending practices, although it's starting to loosen back up! You're going to get your credit pulled. I advise using one of the free credit monitoring platforms that we talked about earlier so you can know your score going in. If you have a 700 credit score you should be a shoe in for most mortgage programs, although I've heard of certain lenders being able to loan to credit scores as low as 580. That's when interviewing three different lenders come into play. You want to know all the details so you can pre-approve yourself. If you know everything they will require, because you've already interviewed multiple lenders, your whole demeanor changes when you walk into the bank. If you know some banks may require last 2 years of W2s/tax returns, and about a month of current paystubs, you can make sure you have those things already. You will want to ask the lender do you have to have a bank account, which most lenders do. If they do require a bank account how much money will you need to have in the account. Some banks require funds to be sourced-and-seasoned. That means you have to have a paper-trail. They want to know where the funds came from (sourced), and depending on the bank the funds have to be in the bank for 3-6 months (seasoned). Depending on what kind of funding program you get they may require you to have 3 months reserves. That's 3xs your monthly payment, and you see that more when you get into investment properties.

Your debt-to-income (DTI) ratio is huge when getting pre-approved by a lender or by yourself. Your dti is the ratio of how much you owe monthly versus how much you make. That's one of those criteria's that vary from bank to bank. This is also one that the immediate loan originator may not know the answer to, you may have to ask to be connected to a supervisor, underwriter, or processor. I've never seen a lender allow you to have more than a 50% dti. When calculating your dti they add up any credit card debt, loans, student loans, car payments, or any other monthly payments you've already committed to. They take that number and divide it by your monthly gross income, times 100. For example, if you make $10,000 a month no more than $5,000 of that can go towards your debts. The mortgage or loan that you are applying for is calculated into that number as well. Continuing with the example above, if you are applying for a $2,000 mortgage you want to make sure your current debts per month are lower than $3,000 because $3,000 plus $2,000 equals 50% dti. The lower your dti the better. Banks don't want to lend you money if you don't have enough cashflow to service the debt.

Now that you've shopped around, and you know which banks require what, if you don't qualify for any of their programs it's always good to shop mortage brokers before you give up. A mortgage broker can be more flexible with their lending because they not only shop your application around locally, but they can shop out of state banks as well. If all the banks in your town require a 680 credit score, a mortgage broker may be able to find a bank that will go as low as 620. Banks have their own money so they can set the bar, either you qualify or you don't. Mortgage brokers can kind of cater to your lower score.

It is critical to be disciplined after you get pre-approved. There are several things that you can do at this pivotal moment that can disqualify you for funding when your application goes to underwriting. Make sure you talk to your lender after you get your pre-approval. This is a step a lot of people forget. They think once they've gotten their pre-approval, they can go buy a car, run up a bunch of credit card debt, take a bunch of money out the bank, or miss a lot of days at work. Have the conversation with your lender. You want to be as transparent and clear about every step as possible. Clarity creates speed, so for this transaction to move swiftly, you want to be upfront about as much as possible. It's not that people lie; it's people often forget. I had a client whose credit score was great, but once he got ran through the CAIVRS report a student loan from 15 years ago popped up. It obviously fell off of his credit report after 7 years, so he didn't think it was an issue. His lender got his FHA converted to a 3% down payment conventional loan so he was still able to close.

House Shopping

Now that you've gotten your pre-approval it's time to start house shopping. In a balanced market I suggest starting to look at houses even before you're pre-approved so you can know what you do and don't want in a house. The Covid market changed everything though. I went to the office and listed a house and had an offer before I made it home, three offers before the first 24 hours. There was a news article about 73 cash offers on a property. It is definitely a seller's market. For that reason, if you're house shopping before your pre-approval do not plan on getting the house you're looking at. There's a good chance by the time you finish getting your application in and the lender issues a pre-approval letter that house will be under contract.

You set your criteria based on how much house you can afford, how many people will be living in the house, how many cars you have, pets, if you need a fenced yard, even age and health can be determining factors when setting your guidelines for a house. It's ok to know exactly what you want and have your non-negotiables, but you want to be broad when telling your agent what type of house you want. If you tell your agent you want a 4-bedroom ranch style house, your agent won't send you a 5-bedroom modern style house, that turns out you would have loved. People don't know what they want until they know what they can have, so start with what you don't want. Most people know exactly what they don't want, but could never tell you what they want. My dream house was on a body of water. Like I mentioned in my perfect day, then I showed a very affordable house on the perfect size body of water. I don't like my dreams being that obtainable so I'm working on a new dream house. Although that water had a loud highway behind it, it was still very affordable. How long you plan on living in the house is a huge factor when figuring out what kind of house you want. If this is going to be your forever home you will want to be pickier, but if you know this is just your first home you have room to be vaguer. All agents have different systems when sending you houses. Typically, after building rapport, your agent will get a feel for what type of house you want and will put you in a CRM. In the CRM it gives the agent the option to send you houses that fit your criteria.

Once the agent sends you a house that you like, you schedule a time to go view it. If you're shopping out of town, or you sick or something and the property doesn't have a 3d tour, your agent may be able to schedule you anyway, and do a zoom, or a video chat from the property. If you are able to go see the house, you want to observe the neighborhood. Are the yards taken care of? Is the street cluttered with cars? Are your neighbors friendly? We had some high-end clients that we even walked around the black with them. You have to get a feel for the house and the neighborhood. Your home is one of the most expensive purchases your will make, so you want to be comfortable in your own home.

Be extremely cognizant when entering other people's house. You have to put yourself in the shoes of the homeowner, because one day you will be that homeowner. They say treat others the way you want to be treated; I say treat others the way they want to be treated. If they take good care of their house, I'm sure they would want you to take consideration when entering their home. If you keep it on the front of your mind, you will have nothing to worry about, because nothing happens by accident, you have to be intentional. It's one of those things that are easy to do, but even easier not to do, so make sure you're respectful.

I wish I could say you will just walk into a house, instantly know it's the one. I wish I could say as soon as you walk in Heaven's gates open, trumpets start playing, and there's going to be a blinding white light. It don't always happen like that, although I went and looked at my house at 10pm at night and was in there for about 2 hours because I liked it so much and didn't want to leave. There's going to be bidding wars, there's going to be contracts falling through for financing, inspection contingencies, repairs, and just disagreements. It's definitely not always a smooth ride, but like I said before if you're honest and up front from the beginning, you will not be at fault. Definitely expect problems to occur. If it was easy the whole world would be homeowners. That's part of that mindset shift, the attitude adjustment, the solutions driven focus I talked about earlier. If you think that it isn't going to be any problems you're dreaming. Motion causes friction, new levels bring new devils, can't get to the promise without the process. Now can it be a smooth transaction? Of course, pay cash and close in 2 weeks, skipping the inspection, with no appraisal, no financing contingency, no lending, not caring how you take over the title, and you still have to hope the seller don't back out. Getting to the next level isn't going to be easy, but you are ready for it, you're built for it. God gives his biggest challenges to his toughest soldier. You can always determine the size of a man by the size of the obstacle it takes to knock him down. As I always say if you can't handle the small problems what will you do when something real happens? If you can't handle an appraisal coming in low, what are you going to do when financing falls through. If you can't handle being outbid on one property, what are you going to do when you have to wait 6 months in order to be in position to purchase your house. I've literally had clients give up after being outbid on their first offer. Their first offer! They had a mortgage and lost to a cash buyer, of course you're going to lose. They gave up and went back to renting. That's fine owning is not for everyone. Continue to rent then. Don't take pride in pulling into your garage when you get home. Don't take pride in taking care of your own lawn. Never build equity, appreciation, get the tax benefits, and never sell your house in 15 years and pay for your kid's college cash, and buy you a smaller house because they moved out.

Putting In An Offer

After you've found a house that you like, now it's time to put your offer in. It's quite simple actually, you will have to decide how much you want to offer and decide how much earnest money you want to put down. What is earnest money? Glad you asked. It's a deposit you make with your offer as a show of good faith. At times it can strengthen your offer. I've heard of buyers putting down over half the asking price as earnest money. You don't have to put down an earnest deposit, it's just showing you have some skin in the game, and you're serious. The earnest money is usually held in an escrow account. Depending on what state you are in, the buyers agent's brokerage can hold it. Earnest money goes towards your closing cost, so if you put down $2,000 of earnest money, that's $2,000 less you have to bring to closing.

I wouldn't ever buy a house without an attorney. A house is one of the biggest purchases we will ever make in our life, so you want to do everything in your power to make sure it is purchased correctly. The attorney will review title work and advice you on how to take ownership. The attorney calculates that earnest money we were just talking about, and any other credit and prorations to make sure you are not over charged for the house. The attorney deals with inspection related issues, they attend the closing, and any legal matters you have. Any contract related questions are directed to an attorney. Even if you didn't know an attorney did these things, failing to plan is planning to fail, so why wouldn't you position yourself in the best way possible to execute this transaction? Your attorney, and their contact info goes on the offer as well.